Things to Make

Written by Peggy R. Greene

Illustrated by Bill Dugan

RANDOM HOUSE 🏠 NEW YORK

Copyright © 1978 by Random House, Inc. All rights reserved under International and Pan-American Copyright Conventions. Published in the United States by Random House, Inc., New York, and simultaneously in Canada by Random House of Canada Limited, Toronto. *Library of Congress Cataloging in Publication Data*: Greene, Peggy R. Things to make. SUMMARY: Contains directions for making toys, presents, and decorations from materials found around the house. 1. Handicraft—Juvenile literature. [1. Handicraft] I. Dugan, William. II. Title. TT160.G82 1981 745.5 80-19639 ISBN: 0-394-83833-5 (B.C.); 0-394-83834-3 (trade); 0-394-93834-8 (lib. bdg.) Manufactured in the United States of America 1 2 3 4 5 6 7 8 9 0

You can have fun making things yourself. With a little help from a bigger person—a parent or older brother or sister—you can make all kinds of toys, presents, and decorations. Look at the pictures in this book to get ideas of your own.

You'll find most of the things you need for Things to Make around your house. *Cardboard cartons and boxes, brown paper bags, paper plates, aluminum cans, egg cartons.*

Drawing paper, construction paper, sticky tape, yarn, plastic-bag twist ties, pipe cleaners, dental floss, string, ribbon, thread.

Pencils, crayons, paints and brushes, paper clips, a stapler, paper reinforcements, scissors, white glue, and paste. Aluminum foil, wooden sticks, buttons, stones, macaroni, salt, flour, eggs, and scraps of fabric and felt. Don't forget to spread out some newspaper where you work. Keep everything you use together in a Things to Make box.

HOW TO TRACE

Here's how to trace a picture from this or any book. Follow the steps in the colored squares. **1.** Cover the picture with white paper and tape it down. Trace the picture with a pencil. **2.** Turn the white paper over and cover the back by scribbling with your pencil. **3.** Turn the white paper over again and tape it to a sheet of heavy construction paper. Use a sharp pencil or ball-point pen to draw over the lines you traced. When you pick up the white paper, the picture will be on the sheet below.

CARDBOARD CARTON TOYS

You will need: large cardboard cartons, rope or strong ribbon, pencils, cardboard or heavy construction paper, crayons, scissors, tape, a stapler, yarn, poster paints, paintbrushes, a grownup.

Bucking Bronco

Carton Train

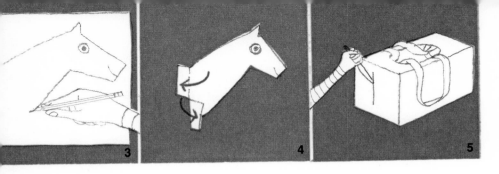

1. Ask a grownup to cut a hole in the top of a large carton so you can fit it over your head and shoulders. 2. Staple rope or strong ribbon to the carton to make shoulder straps. 3. Draw a horse's head on a large sheet of cardboard or heavy construction paper and cut it out. 4. Cut flaps in the horse's neck. 5. Ask a grownup to cut a slit in the carton for you. 6. Push the neck into the slit and tape down the flaps inside the carton. 7. You can staple on yarn to make a horse's mane. You could make a yarn tail, too. Paint a saddle on the carton and ride your Bucking Bronco!

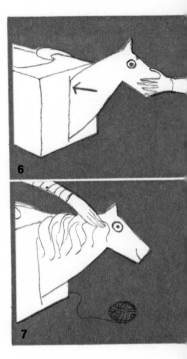

Your Carton Train can have as many cars as you want. Paint cars, windows, wheels, and doors on the sides of the cartons. Line them up, climb inside, and away you go!

NOODLE JEWELRY

Noodles come in all shapes and sizes and they can be painted with poster paints. Noodles with large holes can be strung together with yarn or a long shoelace. To make the elbow macaroni necklace shown, waxed dental floss works best. (Choose the flattest elbows with the largest holes.) **1.** Fold a four-foot length of dental floss in half. Double the two cut ends as shown to make threading easier. **2.** Thread one of the two ends through a noodle. Thread the other end through another noodle. (Use a ball-point pen to help pull the floss through the elbows.) **3.** Push the noodles to the center fold to form a noodle circle. Tie a double knot in the floss. Repeat this step until you have about 2 inches of floss left.

4. Tie the ends to the first circle, put your noodle necklace on, and have a fashion show.

You will need:
assorted noodles with large holes,
elbow macaroni,
yarn or 21-inch shoelaces,
waxed dental floss,
a ball-point pen,
poster paints, brushes.

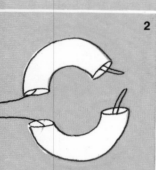

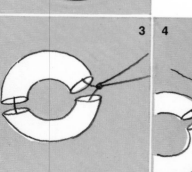

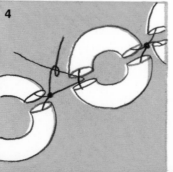

ROCK ART

Rocks and stones can be colorful animals, flowers, or designs. Use them as paperweights, to decorate your room, or give them as presents to someone you love. Pick smooth rocks in all shapes and sizes. Wash them with soap and water. Let them stand overnight to dry.
1. Spread newspaper on the floor. **2.** Use poster paint to cover the whole rock. Let the paint dry thoroughly. **3.** Use a soft pencil to draw a design or a face, feathers, fur, scales, or fins. Use different colored felt-tip pens, or paints and a fine paintbrush, to color in. **4.** When the design is dry, you can give your Rock Art a coat of varnish to make it shine.

You will need: smooth rocks, newspaper, pencils, felt-tip pens, poster paints, paintbrushes, varnish (optional).

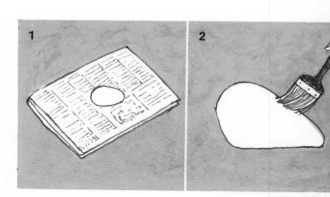

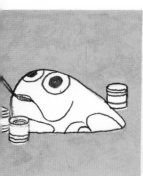

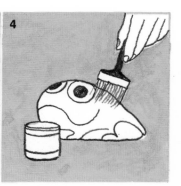

4

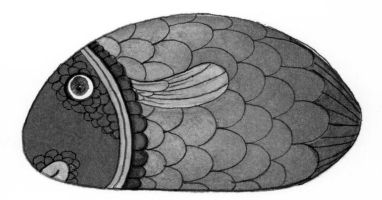

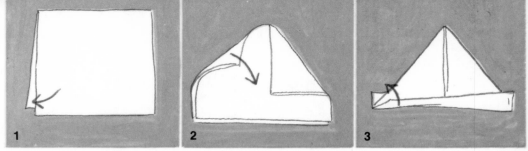

1   2   3

PAPER PLAYTHINGS

You can make hats and toys using heavy construction paper. Follow the steps in the colored squares.

Sailor Hat 1. Fold a large sheet of paper in half. **2.** Fold the top corners down as shown. **3.** Fold up the lower edges and staple.

Helmet 1. Trace around a large pot cover, then cut out the circle you traced. **2.** Cut a pie shape out of the circle as shown. **3.** Tape the ends together. Use a pencil to punch two small holes in the helmet. Tie on two pieces of string or yarn.

You will need: construction paper, a stapler, pencils, a large pot cover, scissors, tape, string or yarn, paper clips, crayons, a small pot cover.

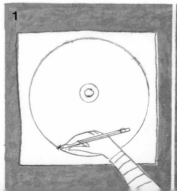

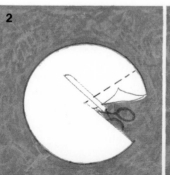

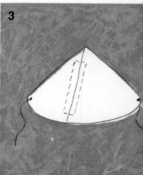

1   2   3

Whirlybird 1. Fold a long strip of paper in half.
(10 by 1½ inches works well.) **2.** Fold one strip
halfway down as shown. Turn over and do the same
to the other strip. **3.** Fasten the bottom with a paper
clip. Drop the Whirlybird and watch it twirl.

Spinning Top 1. Trace around a small pot cover.
2. Cut out the circle you traced. Use crayons to make
a circle design. **3.** Punch a hole through the center
with a pencil and twirl your Spinning Top.

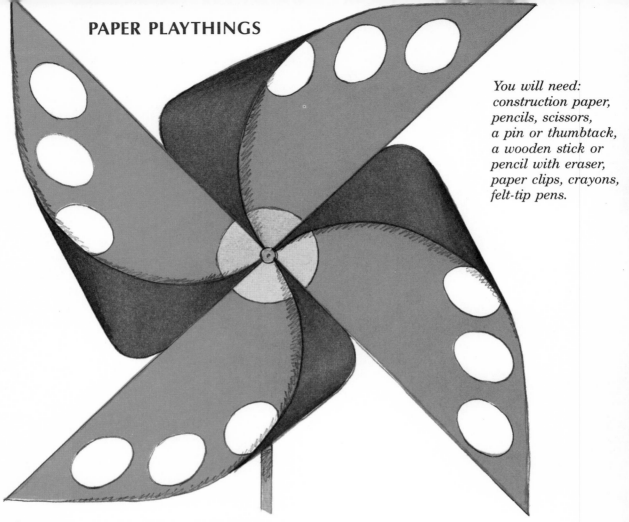

PAPER PLAYTHINGS

You will need: construction paper, pencils, scissors, a pin or thumbtack, a wooden stick or pencil with eraser, paper clips, crayons, felt-tip pens.

Pinwheel 1. On a square sheet of paper the size of this page, draw two straight lines from corner to corner. Draw a small circle in the center and cut four times to the edge of it. **2.** Bend every other corner toward the center as shown. **3.** Push a pin or thumbtack through the center and into a wooden stick or the eraser of a pencil. Your Pinwheel will turn in the wind.

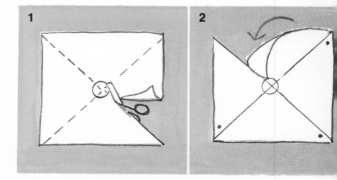

Paper Plane **1.** Fold a sheet of paper in half. **2.** Fold one corner back as shown. **3.** Fold the corner once again. Repeat the steps on the other side. **4.** Fold top edges down. **5.** Put a paper clip on the nose. **6.** Decorate your plane with crayons or felt-tip pens.

PAPER PLATE PLAQUES

Paper Plate Plaques are fun to hang on walls, in windows, or on doors. Use different colored paper plates, or paint them any color you want. Make animals, funny faces, or scary monsters.

You will need: paper plates, pencils, paper reinforcements, assorted buttons, yarn, a large needle, scissors, crayons, poster paints, brushes.

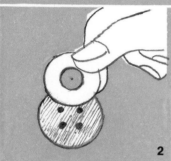

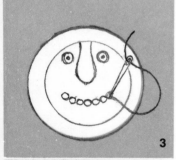

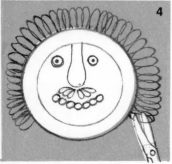

1. With a pencil make a hole in the top of the plate. Put a loop of yarn through the hole so you will be able to hang your plaque. Now draw eyes, a nose, and mouth.
2. Stick paper reinforcements to dark buttons to make the button eyes shown.
3. With a large needle and a length of yarn, sew on eyes and white button teeth.
4. You can make a yarn mustache and hair, too. Use a length of yarn to sew on lots of loops for hair. Snip the loops open with scissors.

HOLIDAY TRIMMINGS

Follow the steps in the colored squares to make your own Holiday Trimmings!

Paper Chains 1. Use colored construction paper or shiny foil wrapping paper. Draw straight lines for strips as shown. Cut out strips. **2.** Tape or paste together to make long chains.

You will need:
colored construction paper or
foil wrapping paper, pencils,
scissors, tape, glue, oranges,
lemons, or limes, toothpicks,
whole cloves, cinnamon, ribbon,
poster paints, brushes, a stapler,
string, aluminum foil, yarn.

Pomander Balls make a room smell nice. Use firm, ripe oranges, lemons, or limes. With a toothpick, prick holes all over the fruit. Push a whole clove into each of the holes. Sprinkle all over with cinnamon. Tie a bright ribbon around the ball and hang in a cool dry place for two weeks.

Flag Chains 1. Paint lots of small flags on sheets of paper, leaving space above each flag. **2.** Cut the flags out and fold as shown. **3.** Tape or staple on a length of string.

Aluminum Balls 1. Make balls of aluminum foil. **2.** Tie a piece of yarn around each ball. Decorate with bright ribbon.

Turn the page for cookie patterns.

COOKIE PATTERNS

You can make a gingerbread man or a holiday horse to hang on your tree. When Mommy is rolling out cookie dough, ask her to roll out some for you. **1.** Trace the man or horse onto a piece of cardboard. (Turn to the beginning of this book to find out how to trace.) Cut out your cardboard pattern and grease it with butter or shortening. **2.** Put your pattern on the dough and cut around it with a blunt-edged knife. Carefully place your cookie on a baking sheet. **3.** Make a small hole in the top of the cookie. Decorate with raisins or nuts, then bake with Mommy's cookies. **4.** When your cookies are cool, you can hang them as they are. Put a loop of yarn through the hole. Or decorate with colored icing.

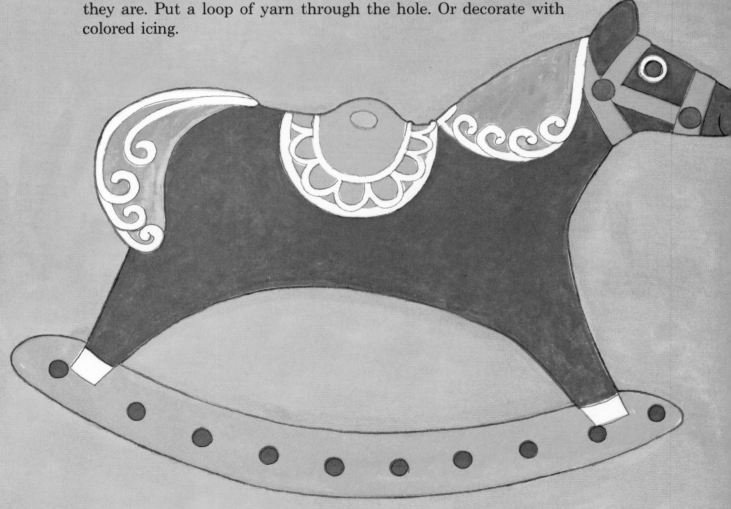

You will need:
cookie dough,
sheets of cardboard,
tracing paper, pencils,
scissors, butter or
shortening, a blunt-edged
knife, a baking sheet,
yarn, a grownup.
Raisins, nuts, colored
icing (optional).

1

2

3

4

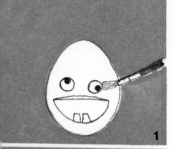

2

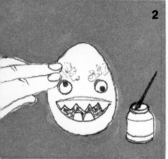

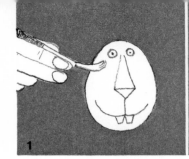

1

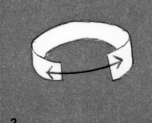

1

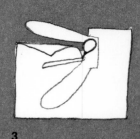

2

3

EGG HEADS

You can make Egg Heads for your Easter basket, or any time!

Funny Egg Head 1. Paint a funny face on a hard-boiled egg. **2.** Trace the teeth on the opposite page, cut them out, and paste to the egg. (Turn to the beginning of this book to find out how to trace.) Paste on bits of cotton for hair.

Bunny Egg Head

1. Paint a bunny face on a hard-boiled egg. **2.** Trace the grass stand. Cut it out, color it in, and tape together. **3.** Trace the bunny ears. Cut them out, color them in, and paste to the egg.

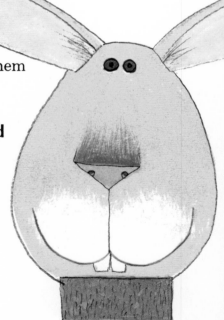

Humpty Dumpty Egg Head

1. Paint a Humpty Dumpty face and a collar and jacket on a hard-boiled egg. **2.** Trace, cut out, and color in arms. Paste them to the egg. **3.** Trace the brick wall. Cut it out, color it in, and fold and tape together as shown.

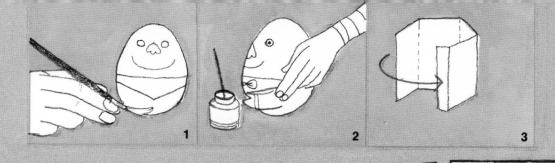

1   **2**   **3**

You will need:
hard-boiled eggs,
pencils, construction paper,
white paper, scissors,
white paste or glue,
crayons, poster paints.

ARMS

TEETH

BRICK WALL

BUNNY EARS

GRASS STAND

EGG CARTON CREATURES

Egg Carton Monster 1. Turn an empty egg carton upside down. Paint it with poster paints. Cut scary teeth from the lid as shown. **2.** Use strips of colored paper or short pieces of yarn for hair. Paste them to the monster's head. **3.** Draw eyes and ears on colored construction paper. Cut them out and paste them on.

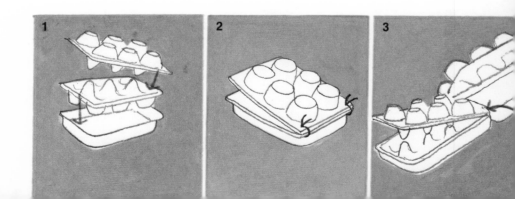

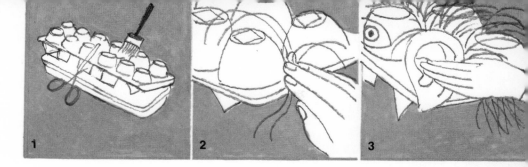

You will need: empty egg cartons, scissors, crayons, construction paper, scraps of yarn, white paste or glue, pencils, poster paints, paintbrushes, long pipe cleaners or large, plastic-bag twist ties.

Egg Carton Crocodile 1. Cut a whole egg carton in half. Glue one half of the bottom into one half of the top as shown. **2.** Use a pencil to punch small holes in both halves of the bottom as shown. Connect the halves by passing long pipe cleaners (or large, plastic-bag twist ties) through the holes. This will be the crocodile's head. **3.** Use a pencil to punch small holes through the corners of several more cartons. (Your crocodile can be as long as you want.) Line them up and tie them together with pipe cleaners or twist ties. **4.** Paint the cartons with poster paints. Draw teeth and eyes on construction paper, cut them out, and paste them on.

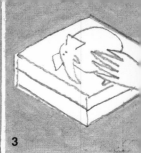

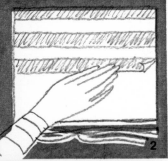

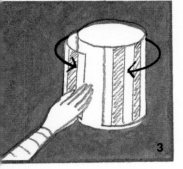

COVERED CANS AND BOXES

Paper-Covered Cans 1. Cut strips of colored construction paper. **2.** Paste the strips on another colored sheet. **3.** Wrap the sheet around a can. Cut off any excess paper and glue to the can.

Ribbon-Covered Cans 1. Measure a length of ribbon. (Grosgrain ribbon and upholstery trim work best.) Make it a little longer than you need to fit around the can. Mark the length and cut. **2.** Cut strips of ribbon the same length as the first. **3.** Paste the ribbon strips on the can as shown.

Covered Boxes 1. Cut out colorful pictures you like from old magazines or greeting cards. **2.** Make a thin paste of white glue and a little water. Use an old brush to spread this paste on a cardboard box. **3.** Put your pictures on the box and give them a few more coats of the thin paste. The paste will dry clear and shiny.

You will need:
aluminum cans,
assorted cardboard boxes,
old magazines or
greeting cards,
colored construction paper,
pencils, white glue, scissors,
ribbon or upholstery trim,
an old paintbrush.

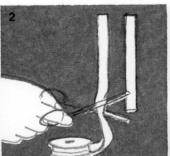

CLAY PLAY

Ask a grownup to help you mix together *4 cups of unsifted flour, 1 cup of salt, and 1½ cups of cold water.* You can knead and model the clay, or roll with a rolling pin and cut out shapes. Let your clay dry overnight before painting. (Or modeled clay can be baked for 1 hour at 325.° Allow model to cool before painting.)

Hand Prints 1. Roll out the clay. It should be ½ inch thick. **2.** Make a print with your hand. **3.** Use a small pot cover to cut a circle around your hand print. Make a hole in the top for hanging. Let your print dry overnight. **4.** Paint with poster paints. (You can give your print a coat of varnish to make it shiny.)

Turtle 1. Make a turtle shape of clay. **2.** Make balls of clay for head and feet. **3.** Wet balls slightly and attach to turtle. **4.** When the turtle is dry, paint with poster paint.

Porcupine Pencil Holder 1. Make a porcupine body of clay. **2.** Stick a pencil into the soft clay to make holes as shown. When the porcupine is dry, paint with poster paints.

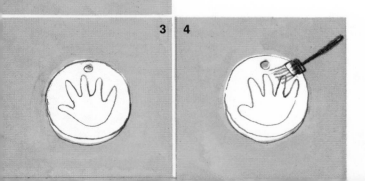

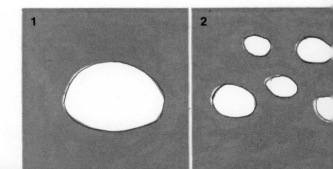

You will need:
clay, a small pot cover,
a rolling pin, a spoon, pencils,
cookie cutters, small cardboard boxes,
candles, poster paints,
varnish (optional), a grownup.

Candle Holder Roll out the clay. It should be almost 1 inch thick. **1.** Use a small cardboard box, a cookie cutter, or a spoon to cut out shapes. **2.** Press a candle into soft clay to make a hole. Let the candle holder dry, then paint with poster paints.

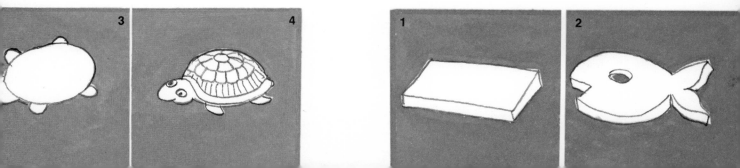

PAPER BAG MASKS

Paper Bag Masks are more fun than masks you buy in the store. Look at the pictures to get ideas of your own.

1. Put a large grocery bag over your head. Ask someone to cut out the sides for shoulder room.
2. Point to your eyes with your finger. Ask someone to make gentle marks with a crayon for eyes. **3.** Lay the bag flat and cut out small holes for eyes. (Be sure you only cut through one side.) Use paper reinforcements around the holes. Use crayons, paints, or felt-tip pens to make a funny face. **4.** Or cut out paper ears and a nose and paste them to the bag.

You can add hair to your paper bag masks. **1.** Draw straight lines on several sheets of colored construction paper and cut into strips. **2.** To make curly hair, wind the strips around your finger. **3.** Bend one end of each strip as shown. **4.** Tape the strips to the top of the bag.

You will need: grocery bags, scissors, paper reinforcements, construction paper, crayons, glue, poster paints or felt-tip pens, tape, another person.

1

2

3

4

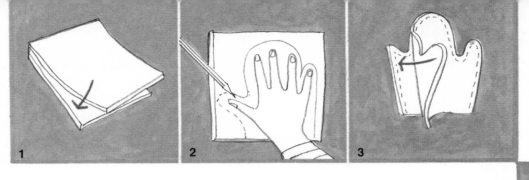

1

2

3

4

5

6

HAND PUPPETS

You can give a puppet show with hand puppets you make yourself. To make the lion puppet shown: **1.** Pin together two pieces of felt or heavy scrap fabric. Lay them on a flat surface. **2.** Trace around your hand to make the puppet shape as shown. (Make sure you leave plenty of space around your hand so it will fit easily into the puppet.) **3.** Cut out the shape you traced. Using a large needle and a length of yarn, sew the two shapes together. Make small stitches near the edge as shown. (Or the shapes can be stapled together with a small stapler.) Make sure you leave the bottom edge open. **4.** Draw a snout shape on a piece of felt or fabric and cut it out. Cut out shapes for eyes, a nose, and a tongue, too. (You can color them in with felt-tip pens.) **5.** Glue on the shapes you traced to make the lion's face. **6.** Use a large needle and a length of yarn to sew lots of loops near the top edge. Snip the loops open with scissors to make the lion's mane.

You will need: pins, felt or heavy scrap fabric, yarn, a large needle, pencils, scissors, felt-tip pens, glue.

YARN WEAVING

A Yarn Weaving looks pretty anywhere you hang it. Your design can have as many colors as you like. Practice weaving on two 12-inch sticks. Then you can make weavings on longer sticks.

1. Using the end of a ball of yarn, tie two sticks together.
2. Loop the yarn around and around the sticks as shown. (Make sure you keep the yarn pulled tight.) When you have a few inches of yarn, you can add a new color. Cut the yarn with scissors and tie the end to the new color in a small, tight knot. Continue looping the new color. (Push all knots to the back of the weaving.) When you fill the sticks, tie a yarn knot around one stick.

To make yarn pompons: 1. Wrap yarn around and around a card as shown.
2. Carefully push the yarn loops off the card and tie tightly in the middle with a few lengths of yarn. Snip the loops open and push the end of the stick through your pompon.

You will need:
2 12-inch wooden sticks,
balls of different colored yarn,
scissors, cardboard.

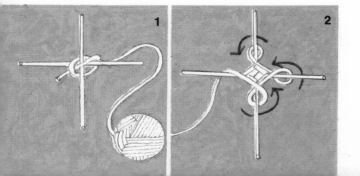

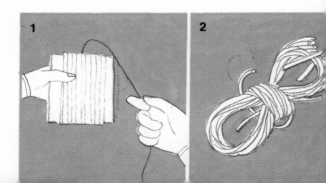